W9-ATR-680

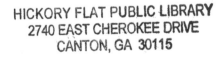

Courteous Kids

Hello

By Janine Amos   Illustrated by Annabel Spenceley

Gareth Stevens Publishing
A WORLD ALMANAC EDUCATION GROUP COMPANY

Please visit our web site at: www.garethstevens.com
For a free color catalog describing Gareth Stevens'
list of high-quality books and multimedia programs,
call 1-800-542-2595 (USA) or 1-800-461-9120 (Canada).
Gareth Stevens Publishing's Fax: (414) 332-3567.

Library of Congress Cataloging-in-Publication Data

Amos, Janine.
      Hello / by Janine Amos; illustrated by Annabel Spenceley.
         p. cm. — (Courteous kids)
      Includes bibliographical references.
      ISBN 0-8368-2803-8 (lib. bdg.)
      1. Conduct of life—Juvenile literature. 2. Salutations—
Juvenile literature. [1. Etiquette. 2. Salutations. 3. Conduct
of life.] I. Spenceley, Annabel, ill. II. Title.
BJ1597.A47   2001
395.1'22—dc21   00-049294

Gareth Stevens editor: Anne Miller
Cover design: Joel Bucaro

This edition © 2001 by Gareth Stevens, Inc. First published by Cherrytree Press,
a subsidiary of Evans Brothers Limited. © 1999 by Cherrytree (a member of the
Evans Group of Publishers), 2A Portman Mansions, Chiltern Street, London
W1M 1LE, United Kingdom. This U.S. edition published under license from
Evans Brothers Limited. Additional end matter © 2001 by Gareth Stevens, Inc.

Printed in the United States of America

1 2 3 4 5 6 7 8 9 05 04 03 02 01

David's Kite

David is going to the park with Dad.

They meet a neighbor.

Dad stops to say "hello."
Mr. Hill says "hello" to Dad and David.

David does not answer.

How does Mr. Hill feel?

Dad reminds David to say "hello."

David thinks about it.

On the way home, they see Mr. Hill again.
This time David remembers.

How does Mr. Hill feel now?

Diane and Juanita

Diane hangs up her coat at school.

Juanita dashes in.
She is excited for class to start.

Diane is happy to see Juanita.

Juanita forgets to say "hello."

How does Diane feel?

Then Juanita remembers.

How does Diane feel now?

Jon Joins In

Jamie and his friends are playing soccer.

Jon walks by and sees them playing.

He wants to join in the game.

Jamie sees Jon watching.

Jamie says "hello" to Jon.

How does Jon feel?

Jon joins in the game.

29

30

31

More Books to Read

Hello! Good-bye! Aliki (Greenwillow)

Manners. Aliki (Greenwillow)

Mind Your Manners. Peggy Parish
   (Mulberry Books)

What Do You Say, Dear? A Book of Manners for All Occasions.
   Sesyle Joslin (HarperTrophy)

Note to Parents and Teachers

The questions that appear in **boldface** type can be used to initiate discussion with your children or class. Encourage them to think of possible answers before continuing with the story.

Additional Resources

Parents and teachers may find these materials useful in discussing manners with children:

Video: *Manners Can Be Fun!* (ETI-KIDS, Ltd.)
   This video includes a teacher's guide.

Web Site: *Preschoolers Today: Where Have the Manners Gone?*
   www.preschoolerstoday.com/resources/articles/manners.htm